POLICE
Search &
RESCUE!
SERVE & PROTECT

Air-Sea Rescue Officers

by Kevin Blake

Consultant: Dan Edling
New York Police Department Aviation Historian
New York, New York

BEARPORT
PUBLISHING

New York, New York

Credits

Cover and Title Page, © num_skyman/Shutterstock, © Dmitry Brizhatyuk/Shutterstock, © Tyler Olson/Shutterstock, and © Richardzz/Shutterstock; 4–5, © Brendan McDermid/Reuters/Corbis; 5, © Bladerunner88/Dreamstime; 6, © Brendan McDermid/Reuters/Corbis; 7T, © Dziekan/Retna Ltd./Corbis; 7B, © Kathy Willens/Associated Press; 8, © Florin Stana/Shutterstock; 9L, U.S. Coast Guard photo by Petty Officer 3rd Class Cory J. Mendenhall - U.S. Coast Guard; 9R, © Brian Finestone/ Dreamstime; 10, © Leungphotography/Dreamstime; 11, Courtesy of NYPD Air-Sea Rescue Aviation Unit; 12, © Tylinek/iStock; 13, © Henny Ray Abrams/Associated Press; 14, © Robcorbett/Dreamstime; 15, © Simon Gruney/Thinkstock; 16, © Crok Photography/Shutterstock; 17T, © Robcorbett/ Dreamstime; 17B, Courtesy of NYPD Air-Sea Rescue Aviation Unit; 18, © Pikul Noorod/Shutterstock; 19T, Courtesy of NYPD Air-Sea Rescue Aviation Unit; 19B, © Peter Armstrong/Dreamstime; 20, © Todd Curabba; 21T, © Andy Jones/The Tampa Tribune; 21B, © Cliff McBride/The Tampa Tribune; 22–23, © Tony Linck/Superstock; 22, © cunaplus/Shutterstock; 23, Courtesy of NYPD Air-Sea Rescue Aviation Unit; 24, © Scott Lomenzo/Shutterstock.com; 25T, © Robert Kalfus; 25B, Courtesy of NYPD Air-Sea Rescue Aviation Unit; 26–27, © Stephen Meese/Shutterstock; 26B, © Heiko Kieral/ Shutterstock; 27T, © Tampa Police Department; 27B, © Liquid Productions, LLC/Shutterstock; 28L, © andrej pol/Shutterstock; 28R, © P_Wei/iStock; 29L, © PhotoObjects.net/Thinkstock; 29TR, © Cesare Andrea Ferrari/iStock; 29BR, © Andrey Nekrasov/Alamy; 31, © Sergio Vila/Dreamstime; 32, © Lissandra Melo/Shutterstock.

Publisher: Kenn Goin
Senior Editor: Joyce Tavolacci
Creative Director: Spencer Brinker
Design: Dawn Beard Creative
Photo Researcher: We Research Pictures, LLC.

Special thanks to Nick Minx and Brian Poplawski for their expert help in reviewing this book.

Library of Congress Cataloging-in-Publication Data

Blake, Kevin, author.
  Air-sea rescue officers / by Kevin Blake.
     pages cm. — (Police : search & rescue!)
  Includes bibliographical references and index.
  ISBN 978-1-943553-12-9 (library binding) — ISBN 1-943553-12-2 (library binding)
  1. Search and rescue operations—Juvenile literature. I. Title.
  TL553.8.B53 2016
  363.34'81—dc23
                          2015033111

For more information, write to Bearport Publishing Company, Inc., 45 West 21st Street, Suite 3B, New York, New York 10010. Printed in the United States of America.

10 9 8 7 6 5 4 3 2 1

Contents

Emergency Landing

On January 15, 2009, an airplane carrying 155 people left New York City's LaGuardia Airport. Minutes after takeoff, the passengers heard loud thuds. The plane had struck a flock of geese, which caused both engines to stop working. Without engines, the plane would soon **plummet** to the ground. The pilot had to make a quick and daring decision—an emergency landing in the nearby Hudson River.

The plane that struck the geese was US Airways Flight 1549.

The pilot carefully steered the plane toward the river and then glided it down. When the plane landed, freezing water poured into the **cabin**. The crew and passengers **evacuated** to the plane's wings, where they waited in the frigid river. With every passing second, the victims were in danger of drowning or freezing to death. The people needed help—and fast. Within minutes, 750 New York Police Department (NYPD) officers were on the scene—including members of the **elite** Air-Sea Rescue Aviation Unit.

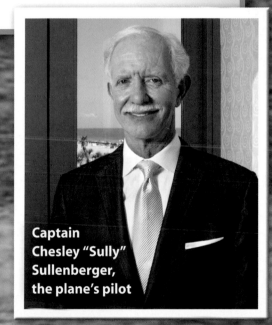

Captain Chesley "Sully" Sullenberger, the plane's pilot

 When the plane crashed into the Hudson River, the water was 36°F (2°C). At that temperature, a person can become **hypothermic** within five minutes.

River Rescue

A crew that included Detectives Michael Delaney and Robert Rodriguez from the NYPD Air-Sea Rescue Aviation Unit flew over the plane **wreckage** in a helicopter. They scanned the river for people in need of immediate help. The detectives quickly spotted a woman who had fallen into the icy water. Wearing special suits designed to protect them in very cold water, they dove from the helicopter into the river and swam to the panicked woman. "She was frightened . . . and very **lethargic**," remembers Detective Rodriguez.

The air-sea police crew and other rescuers wasted no time in helping the passengers and crew of Flight 1549.

Detective Delaney grabbed the woman and began to swim. With powerful strokes, he swam to a nearby rescue boat. When they reached the boat, rescue workers pulled the cold, frightened woman safely aboard. After the rescue, the detectives said they weren't heroes. "It's just another jump out of the helicopter for us!"

Detective Robert Rodriguez (left) with his partner, Detective Michael Delaney (right)

An NYPD rescue boat in the Hudson River

Because of the brave work of the air-sea unit and the other rescuers, all 155 people aboard Flight 1549 survived the crash landing.

Where Others Can't Go

Why is there a need for air-sea rescue officers? Sometimes, people might become stranded in an icy river like the crew and passengers of Flight 1549. They could also become **adrift** in the ocean or lost on top of a steep mountain or in another hard-to-reach place. That's when the brave members of air-sea rescue police are called into action.

A hiker stuck on a mountain in a snowstorm

Using helicopters, boats, and other specialized equipment, air-sea rescuers can get to places where other police officers cannot. These highly skilled individuals are ready for duty 24 hours a day. They are prepared to work in dangerous conditions, such as in rough seas or in stormy skies. Every day, air-sea rescuers risk their own lives to help people in need.

It isn't just police officers who perform air-sea rescues. The United States Coast Guard and local fire departments also help rescue people at sea and in other places that are difficult to access.

U.S. Coast Guard helicopter

Fire department boat

LIFEGUARD

The U.S. Coast Guard works together with the Los Angeles County Fire Department to perform an air-sea rescue.

Air-sea rescue officers help locate people who may be lost or seriously injured and carry them to safety.

9

In the Air

At a small airport called Floyd Bennett Field in Brooklyn, New York, eight police helicopters sit on a runway. This is where the NYPD's Air-Sea Rescue Aviation Unit is based. The helicopters and rescuers are ready to take off at a moment's notice in case there is an emergency in or around New York City.

Floyd Bennett Field in Brooklyn, New York

There are usually four or more crewmembers on each helicopter. They include a pilot, a co-pilot or **crew chief**, and two rescue swimmers or **scuba** divers. All of the crewmembers are experienced police officers who have trained extensively to learn how to operate a rescue helicopter. The crew also receives nearly a year of training in rescue operations, such as how to use a **hoist** and **rappel** from a moving **chopper**. More importantly, they learn to be prepared for any emergency, day or night.

The inside of an NYPD helicopter cockpit

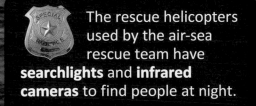
The rescue helicopters used by the air-sea rescue team have **searchlights** and **infrared cameras** to find people at night.

In the Water

Training to become a swimmer or diver in an air-sea rescue unit is especially challenging. In many states, a police officer needs to first pass a **grueling** physical test. The officer must be able to do 12 pull-ups, 32 pushups, then run a mile (1.6 km) in a short period of time. That's not all. He or she is also required to swim 500 yards (457 m) in 12 minutes.

Sometimes the water can be so murky that "you can't see your hand in front of your face," according to one NYPD diver.

Being incredibly fit helps police rescue swimmers and divers stay afloat in rough seas and in rivers with fast-moving **currents**. Divers must also be strong enough to carry up to 80 pounds (36 kg) of gear during some rescue missions. The equipment includes **sonar**, cameras, metal detectors, and knives to cut through seat belts to free people from sunken cars.

Police divers look for missing swimmers in the Atlantic Ocean.

The Harbor Police Department in San Diego, California, has 20 full-time divers. It's one of the largest police dive teams in the country.

Teamwork

For a rescue to be successful, flight crews, swimmers, and divers need to work in **unison**. That's why air-sea rescue units train together. They practice dangerous rescues in order to prepare for the real thing. In one **drill**, a diver jumps into the water from a helicopter and is then rescued by other divers.

Members of the NYPD's Air-Sea Rescue Aviation Unit during a drill

Crews even prepare for what to do if things go terribly wrong with a rescue. In 2010, air-sea rescuers trained for a situation in which the police helicopter was forced to **abandon** its divers in the water far from shore. The divers immediately dropped bright green dye in the water to **signal** their location to passing airplanes or choppers. Then, when no rescuers appeared, they began the long swim to shore. To keep from getting too tired, they swam on their backs while kicking their long **fins**.

Police divers use swim fins to help them move farther and faster in the water.

fins

Besides using brightly colored dye, divers can also signal their location in the water by using mirrors to reflect the sun's light back into the sky.

Search and Locate

Often, air-sea rescue crews spend a lot of time searching for a person in need of rescue. That's what happened in the summer of 2014 when two men got thrown off their jet skis near Staten Island, New York. A tugboat operator quickly found one of the men, but the other man remained missing.

Jet skis are small boats that skim along the surface of the water.

The NYPD Air-Sea Rescue Aviation Unit began an **aerial** search of the water. From aboard the helicopter, the officers carefully checked the area for any sign of the missing jet skier. The search lasted many hours. Finally, the crew chief spotted a man waving his arms on a small island. "There he is! There he is!" the officer yelled. Another officer was lowered down from the helicopter. He grabbed the jet skier and both men were hoisted up to the chopper.

An NYPD helicopter searches New York Harbor near Staten Island.

The small island where the missing man was found

The missing jet skier swam to a small **deserted** island that was no bigger than half a football field.

Nighttime Save

Sometimes, air-sea rescuers have to use their skills in total darkness. Late one night in 2002, NYPD air-sea rescuers got a call from a fisherman who was far out to sea and very sick. His boat was almost 20 miles (32 km) from land. Without immediate help, the fisherman could die.

Air-sea rescuers are ready to help at any hour of the night.

An NYPD helicopter sped through the night sky until the crew finally spotted the fisherman's boat floating in the dark ocean. "All you see is black ink out there," said the pilot. The helicopter **hovered** about 60 feet (18 m) above the boat. The crew chief, Patrick Corbett, carefully lowered a special basket and a crewmember down to the fisherman, who had become **unconscious**. Then the man was loaded into the basket and pulled up to the helicopter. The NYPD rushed him to a hospital, saving his life.

Air-sea rescuers often use a piece of equipment called a Stokes basket to lift people into helicopters.

Stokes basket

The fisherman was rescued with a Stokes basket similar to this one.

A Horrible Crash

Occasionally, air-sea rescuers just happen to be in the right place at the right time. Officers Dave Dennison and Brian Gentry were in a helicopter on a nighttime **patrol** in Tampa, Florida, when they heard a pilot's call for help over the radio. Then, in the distance, the officers saw the pilot's plane **nose-diving** toward the ground in a ball of flames. Within a few seconds, the small plane had crashed into a field near the Tampa International Airport.

A Tampa Police Department helicopter

Most helicopters can fly as fast as 145 miles per hour (233 kph).

Officers Dennison and Gentry raced their helicopter toward the wreckage, arriving moments after the crash. Once on the ground, they found the pilot unconscious and pinned against his seat. They carefully removed the man from the twisted metal and gave him **first aid** until more help arrived. After the rescue, Tampa's mayor said, "It was an amazing act of bravery."

The officers pulled the crash victim from the crushed plane, saving his life.

Officers Dave Dennison and Brian Gentry

A Daring Rescue

Air-sea rescuers are always ready to help out, even if that means assisting other teams with a rescue. In May 2014, Amanda Graham was hiking with her family in New Jersey. Suddenly, she slipped and tumbled down a steep cliff. "There was a really loud snap," Amanda remembers. It was her ankle breaking. Her family called 9-1-1, and local firefighters soon arrived to help.

The high cliffs of Palisades Interstate Park near the Hudson River where Amanda Graham got hurt

Amanda Graham broke two bones in her ankle. "I was honestly afraid when I looked down that I was going to see bone," Amanda remembers.

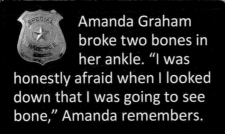

To reach Amanda, 20 firefighters hiked 1,640 feet (500 m) up a dangerous trail. After they reached her, they looked around for a way to get her off the cliff. Carrying Amanda down would be impossible. "It's a steep drop," one fireman said. The firefighters knew exactly who would be able to help—the NYPD Air-Sea Rescue Aviation Unit.

Saved!

An NYPD helicopter sped to the scene of the accident. The pilot and other officers saw the tall, steep cliffs and knew it would not be an easy rescue. The pilot flew the helicopter alongside the cliff and hovered about 50 feet (15 m) above Amanda. Then, while he kept the helicopter steady, the hoist operator lowered Officer Edgar Burroughs down to the injured hiker.

A police helicopter races across the Hudson River toward Palisades Interstate Park.

Each rescue helicopter carries medical supplies and can serve as an airborne ambulance for people who are ill or injured.

"We were battling . . . mud, slippery rocks, and we were 200 feet (61 m) above the Hudson River," said Officer Burroughs. Once on the cliff, he carefully placed the injured hiker in a Stokes basket. Amanda stayed calm even though she was afraid. The officers slowly and carefully hoisted her into the chopper. Thanks to their expert training and teamwork, the rescue was a success.

After being rescued, Amanda was treated for her broken ankle at a nearby hospital.

The NYPD crew that rescued Amanda

An Animal in Danger

You don't have to be a human being to be saved by a police air-sea rescue crew. In Tampa, Florida, members of the police **marine** unit received a call that an eight-month-old puppy was trapped in the nearby Hillsborough River. Police officers rushed to the scene to try to save the dog.

The Hillsborough River in Florida where the puppy was trapped

The Hillsborough River is home to many wild animals, including American alligators, which sometimes attack pets.

When they arrived, the officers found more than just the pup. A large marine mammal called a manatee was swimming very close to the struggling dog. According to the officers, it looked as though the manatee was watching over and protecting the puppy.

Officer Randy Lopez jumped into the water and offered the dog treats to **lure** it closer. He was then able to grab the dog and pull it out of the water. It doesn't matter who you are: if you are in danger, you can count on the heroes of police air-sea rescue units!

Officer Randy Lopez with the rescued puppy

After the dog was rescued, the manatee swam away.

Air-Sea Rescue Officers' Equipment

Air-sea rescue officers use special equipment when working. Here is some of their gear.

A **police rescue helicopter** has a special hoist designed to lower an officer down to a victim and lift them both to safety.

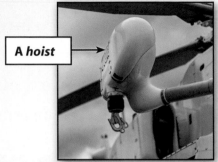

A **hoist**

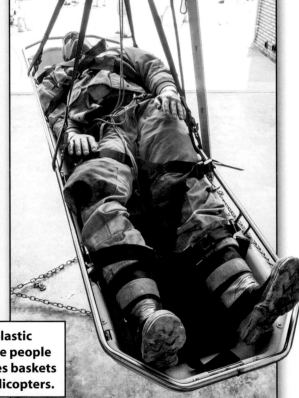

A **Stokes basket** is a metal or plastic stretcher that is used to rescue people in hard-to-reach places. Stokes baskets are typically lowered from helicopters.

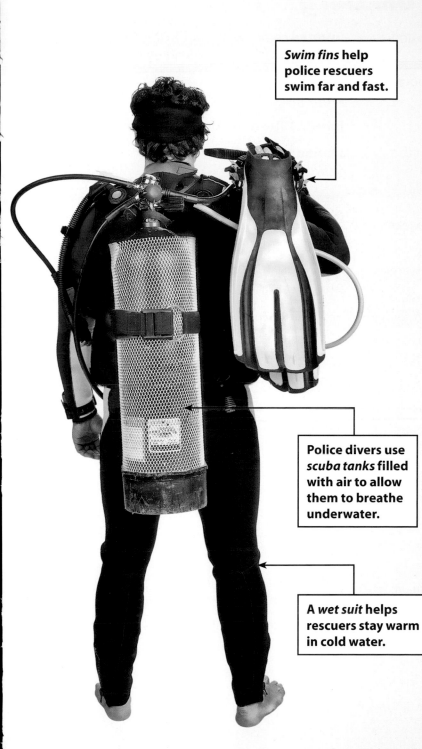

Swim fins help police rescuers swim far and fast.

A *diving knife* allows a police diver to cut through nets or other obstacles in the water.

Police divers use *scuba tanks* filled with air to allow them to breathe underwater.

A *wet suit* helps rescuers stay warm in cold water.

An *underwater metal detector* can help a police diver find a sunken car or other metal object in the water.

Glossary

abandon (uh-BAN-duhn) to leave alone and uncared for

adrift (uh-DRIFFT) floating in water without control of the direction

aerial (AIR-ee-uhl) from the sky

cabin (KAB-in) the main enclosed part of the airplane where the passengers sit

chopper (CHOP-ur) a helicopter

crew chief (KROO CHEEF) the leader of a team of air-sea rescuers

currents (KUR-uhnts) the movement of water in an ocean or river

deserted (di-ZUHR-tid) having no people living in an area

drill (DRIL) an exercise or activity that is practiced over and over

elite (i-LEET) highly skilled

evacuated (i-VAK-yoo-*ate*-id) moved away from a dangerous area

fins (FINZ) special webbed equipment placed on a swimmer's foot to make him or her swim faster

first aid (FURST AYD) care given to an injured or sick person in an emergency before he or she is treated by a doctor

grueling (GROO-uh-ling) very hard, difficult, or tiring

hoist (HOYST) part of a helicopter used to lift someone up using a rope or cable

hovered (HUHV-urd) floated in place in the air

hypothermic (*hye*-puh-THUR-mik) a condition in which a person's body temperature has become dangerously low

infrared cameras (in-fruh-RED KAM-ur-uhz) cameras that detect heat energy and process it as images

lethargic (LETH-ar-jik) very tired and weak

lure (LOOR) to tempt an animal closer

marine (muh-REEN) something that has to do with the sea

nose-diving (NOZE-dive-ing) an object falling from the sky with its front falling first

patrol (puh-TROHL) to watch or travel around an area to protect it

plummet (PLUM-it) to fall quickly from the sky

rappel (ruh-PEL) to climb down from a higher point using ropes or cables

scuba (SKOO-buh) diving equipment that lets a person breathe underwater; *scuba* stands for *self-contained underwater breathing apparatus*

searchlights (SURCH-lights) high-powered lights on the front of a vehicle used to find a missing person or thing

signal (SIG-nuhl) to try to get someone's attention

sonar (SOH-nar) technology used to locate objects underwater

unconscious (uhn-KON-shuhss) not awake; unable to think, hear, feel, or see

unison (YOO-nuh-suhn) to work together as one

wreckage (REK-ihdj) pieces that remain after something has been badly damaged

Bibliography

Goodman, J. David. "New York City Police Helicopter Rescues Injured Hiker," *The New York Times* (May 13, 2014).

Morelli, Keith. "Police Rescue Pilot after Tampa Airport Crash," *The Tampa Tribune* (December 20, 2013).

Wilson, Michael, and Al Baker. "A Quick Rescue Kept Death Toll at Zero," *The New York Times* (January 15, 2009).

Read More

Aronin, Miriam. *Highway Patrol Officers (Police: Search & Rescue!)*. New York: Bearport (2016).

Ollhoff, Jim. *Search & Rescue (Emergency Workers)*. Minneapolis, MN: ABDO (2013).

Oxdale, Chris. *Air-Sea Rescue.* Glasgow, Scotland: HarperCollins UK (2013).

Learn More Online

To learn more about air-sea rescue officers, visit
www.bearportpublishing.com/PoliceSearchAndRescue

Index

About the Author

Kevin Blake lives in Providence, Rhode Island, with his wife, Melissa, and son, Sam. He hopes he never needs the services of an air-sea rescue team!